Other Books in This Series

Better Baseball for Boys
Better Basketball for Boys
Better Bowling for Boys
Better Football for Boys
Better Physical Fitness for Boys
Better Physical Fitness for Girls
Better Water Skiing for Boys

BETTER GOLF

for Boys

BY THE EDITORS OF *GOLF DIGEST*

DODD, MEAD & COMPANY · New York

1961

Library of Congress Catalog Card Number: 65-13512

Printed in the United States of America

CONTENTS

INTRODUCING THE GAME OF GOLF

It has often been said that golf can be played by anyone from eight to eighty years of age. This is no exaggeration, because golfers over eighty are not unusual, and many past and present champions started swinging a golf club as early as three years.

The fact is that golf is a game that anyone can play and have fun with at the same time. For young boys it will provide many hours of enjoyment, fresh air, exercise, and the opportunity to learn lessons useful all the rest of their lives.

The object of golf is perhaps the most simple of any popular sport—to get a golf ball from the tee into the hole on each of eighteen holes. The number of strokes taken to get the ball to the hole is the player's score on that hole. The total of scores for all eighteen holes makes a round.

If you can swing a baseball bat or a tennis racket, you can learn to hit a golf ball properly. The movements in a golf swing are really not hard. Skill and low scores come in learning to control the arc and power of the swing.

Learning and playing golf are easier for boys

A golf course, such as Oakland Hills Country Club, Birmingham, Mich., is many times the size of a football field. Each hole is different, with mowed and unmowed grass, trees, water, and sand.

today than ever before. This is because more towns have golf courses where beginners can play. Golf clubs and other equipment are better and, at least for beginners, cheaper than before. More professionals offer junior classes where youngsters can get started.

For men and women, boys and girls, golf has become especially popular in the last ten years. Close to ten million Americans play at least a few rounds each year at about 7,500 courses. Almost every town big enough to have its own high school probably has a golf course nearby.

Golf, however, is not a young game. In its present form, but with more primitive equipment, it was played by kings and queens in Scotland at least 500 years ago. The oldest continuous national tournament, the British Open, was first held in 1860.

America's discovery and rapid development of golf came much later. Our first golf courses were built in the 1880's. Even up through World War II ending in 1945 few boys could get close to a golf course unless they were caddies. Caddying is still a fine way to learn golf and earn spending money at the same time, but it is not the only way of getting to play.

Learning golf as a boy will give you a head start that may someday enable you to be a champion. But learning while young is different from learning when you are an adult.

For instance, your muscles are more flexible yet not nearly so strong as they will be later. You will naturally try to swing too hard, and at first you will be wild. You probably won't have much money to spend on new clubs, greens fees, or club dues, but the pictures of a boy your age and the instruction in this book should help you get a better start. Read the text carefully to get the fundamentals firmly in mind. Then practice them faithfully. The results, when you get out on a course, should please and surprise you.

The growth of golf among youngsters is reflected in this typical junior class of beginners being taught by a professional.

All ready for a round, this player is equipped with a bag of clubs and wears comfortable clothing.

HOW TO SELECT THE RIGHT EQUIPMENT

If you are going to start playing golf, you need some basic equipment right away. Probably you are not in a position to go out and buy a new set of clubs and several new balls. Where do you get them then?

The most likely source is your father, older brother, a close friend or relative who already plays the game. If you show him you are eager to learn, he will probably either lend or give you a few of his older pieces of equipment. Then even if no one will give you any balls, you can buy a few in a sporting-goods store for as little as 25 cents each for slightly used ones.

The same store may also sell you a few golf clubs if none are available in your family or from the pro at your local course. But first ask the pro if he has some old clubs that you can buy or rent cheaply.

Chances are your first clubs won't be your last by a long shot. You probably won't have much choice as to the brand or size of clubs you get, unless you save your money to buy a good matched set before you reach high school. Your original equipment won't matter much. The main thing is to learn how to swing and then practice until you are good enough to take advantage of fine clubs.

The maximum number of clubs a player is allowed to carry is fourteen. For a golf professional, this usually includes three or four woods, irons numbered two through nine, each with a different loft to hit the ball different distances, a heavy "wedge" to get a ball out of deep grass and sand, and a putter.

As a beginner, though, you won't need this many clubs to learn the game. The junior beginner's set should include at least a number one wood (driver) to use off the tee, a number three wood (spoon) to hit the ball for distance off the fairway, a three, five, seven, and nine iron and a putter. These seven clubs will be adequate for all the shots you have to make until you can shoot below 100 for eighteen holes.

If possible, get the two woods and four irons about the same relative weight, or matched. Many club manufacturers make these small sets especially for juniors, and at reasonable prices. But remember that it is better to get a good used set of clubs rather than a poor quality new set from a discount store. Avoid cheap clubs because the grips start coming off or the chrome on the irons soon begins to chip.

Another advantage of better-made clubs, even used ones, is that they are sold in several weights and types of grips. So rather than buy one set of clubs and then another as you grow bigger and improve, junior clubs, perhaps a little too long and a little too heavy, are your best buy right now.

If, however, you start out with used adult clubs, they may be much too long and heavy unless you are big for your age. But if you grip down on them a little—just as you "choke" up on a baseball bat—

A source of knowledge about golf clubs and what kind to buy is a golf club professional.

you will learn how to control them. Meanwhile, swinging heavy clubs is a fine way to develop your golf muscles faster.

The kind of putter you use is less important than selecting your other clubs. If you go into a pro shop at a golf course, or into a store that sells clubs, you will see a rack of many kinds of putters. The grips and the heads will be different colors and shapes. Since putting is almost a game within a game, the best putter for you is the one that feels the best to you. This one will get the ball in the hole the most often. Many good golfers keep changing putters. Others have used the same putter since they started playing golf, even as young as you are.

If you have a chance to choose your clubs, try the grip of each one. See if you can wrap your hands around it easily. It will feel smaller than a baseball bat, and even smaller than a broom handle. That's okay. Unless your hands are extra small, the grip should fit into the palms of your hands.

Now for one further bit of advice about balls: all of them, even those made by the same company, are not the same. They all feel hard, but some are made softer on the inside than others. They will compress more easily so you don't have to hit them as hard to get good distance. This "lower compression" type is the kind to get if you can.

Clubs and a ball are obviously essentials, but other pieces of equipment are necessary, too.

First, you need some kind of bag for carrying the

Golf shoes, with special spikes to grip the ground while you swing, are important equipment.

clubs. Your best choice is a lightweight, colorful plastic-and-leather bag that will last several years with good care. A good selection can usually be found at the same store or golf shop where you bought your clubs.

Even the cheapest bag should have a pocket on the outside to hold balls and tees; one or more straps or dividers inside to separate the woods and iron clubs and keep them from banging and denting one another; and a solid bottom that will not sag from the weight of the clubs and which will resist moisture. Bigger and better bags have extra pockets for sweaters, hoods to protect your clubs when you are traveling, and many other features not important to you right now.

If you have new clubs you should have head covers for your woods. These are just leather or plastic mitts with matching numbers. They protect your wooden clubs from scratches and moisture.

Golfers don't wear any standard uniform as football or baseball players do. The best clothes to wear are those most fit for the weather. Since the upper part of the body must turn in swinging a golf club, a stretchy shirt or sweater is best. So is a cap with a bill, to keep either the sun or rain out of your eyes.

The one essential item to wear on the golf course is a pair of shoes with spikes. Your shoes should fit well because when you play eighteen holes you walk a good four miles and you don't want blisters. Spikes keep you from slipping when you swing. A regular pair of leather-soled shoes or sneakers aren't good for golf.

But whether or not you have all the items discussed above is not important right now. As you learn more about the game, you can carefully choose your equipment one piece at a time.

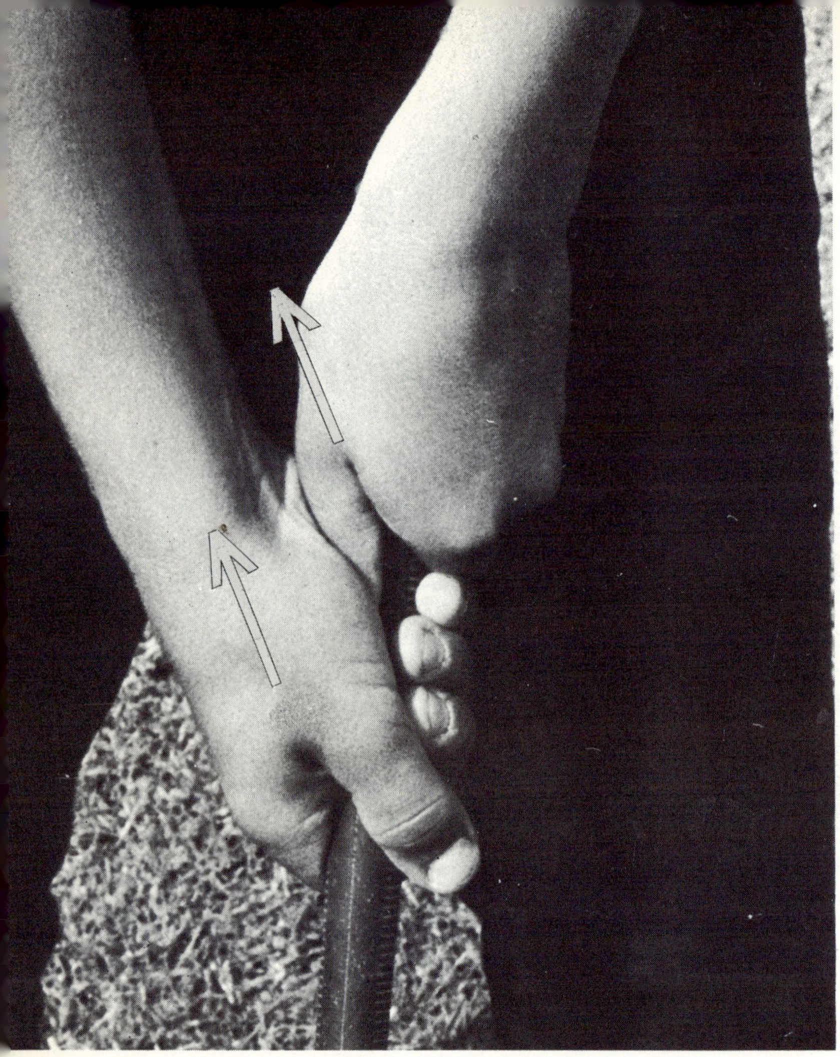

This is the proper grip on the club as the player sees it. Notice how the "V's" of both hands point up right arm.

LEARNING HOW TO SWING

Like most other games, golf can be learned and played well by first understanding a few simple procedures. If you learn them right from the start, and practice them faithfully, you will soon hit a golf ball far and straight.

The three basic elements of the game are you, the club, and the ball. In order to make a good shot you must have a good grip on the club, take a solid, balanced stance, and swing smoothly. To swing right, you must hold the club right and stand right, so let's start at the beginning.

A correct grip on a golf club is a little different from any grip you used before. It's not like in baseball, where you wrap all your fingers and thumbs around the bat handle. It's not like carrying a suitcase or sweeping the porch.

The standard method of gripping a golf club lets both hands work as a tcam. When your hands fit and move well with the club, swinging at the ball becomes simple. Here's how you form the grip.

Take a golf club and stand it up in front of you. Put your left hand under the handle of the club near the end. Keep the palm open. With the arm hanging down in a natural position, the fingers will be pointed out to the right. The thumb is out to the left. With the club lying across the palm, just wrap your left hand around it. The thumb thus ends up on top of the club handle, pointed down the shaft. Your left hand is then all set.

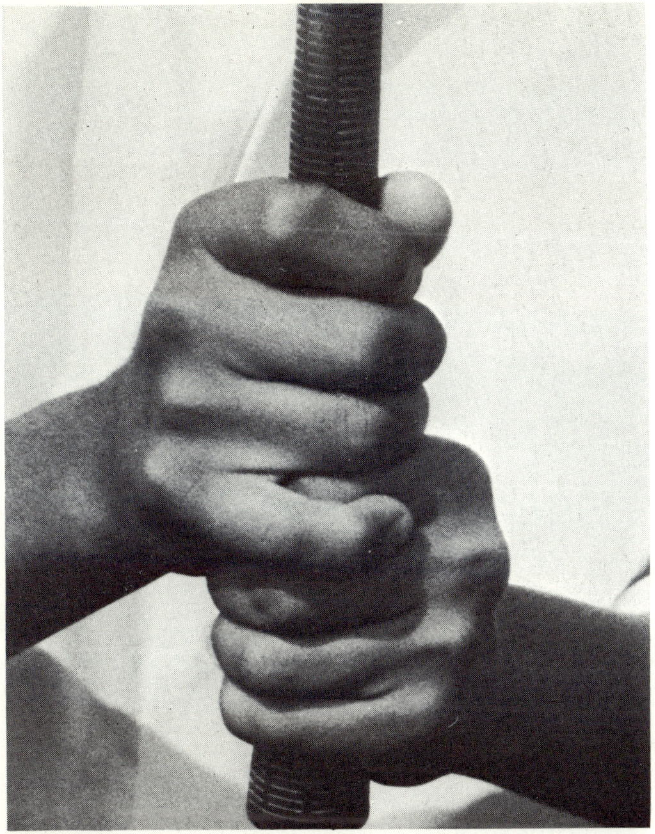

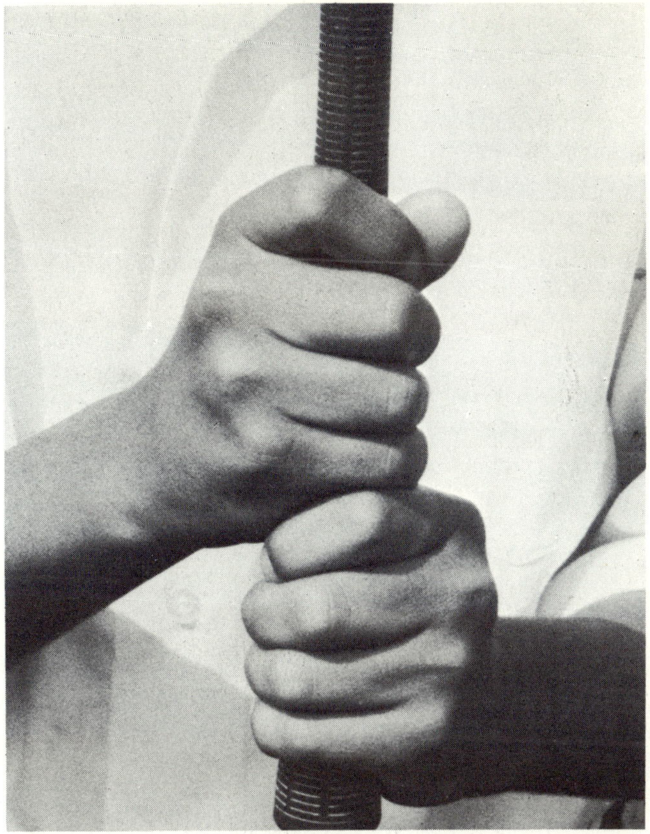

The underside of the grip, as seen from underneath, shows two ways of holding on. At left, little finger of right hand is overlapped. At right, all fingers are on club—a method helpful to many junior players for added strength.

Now for the right hand. Just as on a baseball bat, the right hand is placed closer to the hitting end of the golf club. But the little finger of the right hand must be across the first finger of the left hand and into the crack next to the second finger of the left hand. The club will then be across the right palm as it was in the left hand. The first three right fingers wrap around the club and the right thumb comes up almost on top, with the left thumb underneath it. The cracks between the thumbs and first fingers should point up to the right shoulder.

Feel funny? It should, because it is unique to golf. Called the overlapping grip, it was developed around 1900 by a great British champion, Harry Vardon. A few other variations have been tried and even used by some champion players, but no one has ever really improved on this grip.

Don't squeeze the club tight in your palms. The golf club is held mostly by the fingers. Be firm with the last three fingers of your left hand and the middle two fingers of your right hand. This will help the hands work together, give the grip power, and keep it from becoming stiff.

Remember: your only contact with the golf club is through the hands. The grip must be right or all is lost from the beginning.

Now you are ready to take a stance. Getting set to hit a shot is called addressing the ball. But let's forget the ball for now.

This is how the player looks as he stands ready to hit a shot with a wood. Ball is opposite left heel and line across feet points in same direction as direction of hole. Variations in stance will help the player hook with right foot pulled back or slice with left foot pulled back.

With the club in your hands, hold it down in front of you with the clubhead on the ground. Spread your feet apart a little way, about a foot of distance between your shoes. Your toes shouldn't be pointed straight ahead, but rather turn out to the side at slight angles.

Are your arms hanging down straight in front of you? They shouldn't be against your body and you shouldn't be leaning forward on your toes, either. Bend your knees just a little and feel as if you were going to sit down on a stool behind you.

Now here's a test. Have someone give you a gentle push from the front, then from the back. Do you fall off balance too easily one way or the other? Make sure you have your weight divided equally on both feet, and between your heels and your toes.

Now with the club out in front of you, look down at your arms. The left arm should be straight right through the wrist, forming a line that goes on down the club to where the ball will bc. The right arm, starting with a slight bend at the wrist, comes away to leave a V-shaped space in between the arms. The right elbow is bent a little and pointed toward the ground.

Before you start swinging there's one thing to keep in mind. The head is the center of a golfer's game. The swing revolves around it almost like the earth turning on its axis. You must start with your head and eyes steady over the ball, and try to keep the head there until after the ball is hit.

The swing itself is not a bit complicated if you have your hands and body in the right position. Before attempting it with a club, try this exercise. Take a ball in your right hand, stand in a golf position, and throw the ball underhand across in front of you. Can you get the feel of that smooth back, down, and through motion? That's the way a good golf swing should feel.

Now try it with a golf club. As you take the club back, turn a bit to the right at the waist. Your hands should come up to about shoulder height. There the wrists will be fully bent or cocked and the club will be pointing straight back over the back of your neck. Your left knee will be pointed at your right knee. Your head should still be straight over the ball. The right elbow must be kept down and pointed to the ground.

All of these things should happen naturally and together. If you swing correctly you won't havc to think about anything, but here are some good checkpoints to watch.

The backswing should be slow and smooth. There is no pause at the stop, just a movement in the opposite direction. Now you are ready to hit the ball.

Coming down your arms move a little faster. Eventually, when you have learned how to swing properly, the down stroke will work so easily you won't have time to think about it.

Two things happen together in coming down correctly. Much of your weight that has turned onto your right side on the backswing shifts back to the left side. At the same time the left shoulder and arm pull the club back down toward the ground.

It is important that the wrists keep cocked until the club head approaches the ball. Then they unwind, just as your wrist snaps when you throw a baseball. Letting loose at the last minute gives the stroke extra power.

This brief discussion of what happens during a good golf swing should serve as an introduction to making actual shots. We will go into more detail in the next five chapters. But intense work on the basic grip, stance, and swing will make the individual shots come easier.

HOW TO HIT THE TEE SHOT

In golf the equivalent of a home run or a long touchdown pass is the booming drive off the tee.

All the great golf champions, such as Arnold Palmer and Jack Nicklaus, make the game look easy because they hit such long tee shots. A good drive starts the golfer out right and gives him a mental lift.

A long, straight hit off the tee calls for a long, straight-faced club with a big hitting surface. This is where the woods come in, particularly the number one wood. This is the driver, which you must master in order to be a good golfer. At the beginning you may want to use your number three wood for tee shots because it has a more slanted face that helps get the ball into the air easier. That's fine for now, but don't adopt a permanent substitute for the driver.

The first shot on a hole, whether you use a number one wood or some other club, is different from the rest in one important way. This is the only time you are allowed to use a little wooden tee. Take advantage of this allowance in the rules. Tee your ball up at least an inch or so off the ground every time you start a hole.

First pick out a level spot on which to tee up the ball. On a mat at a driving range there is obviously no problem. But if you are on either grass or dirt pick a spot where the club won't hit either a hole or a bump behind the ball. Also, at the golf course, make sure you are teeing up within two club lengths in an area behind the tee markers.

Once the ball is sitting up there on the tee, stand about where you will be when you actually get ready to hit the ball. First make sure, though, that your feet won't either be in a hole or on a slippery spot. If you can't get a good stance, convenient to your ball, move the teed ball to another spot.

Ready to hit the ball now? Not quite. Decide first where you want to hit it. In golf, accuracy is more important than distance, even off the tee. Always try to keep the ball in the fairway. So try to pick out a spot, using a tree or post in the distance to aim for.

Next, take the club in your hands. Get the grip right before you stand up to the ball. Remember to hold the club firmly with the fingers. The V's formed by the thumb and first finger on each hand should be aiming up at your right shoulder. The right little finger should be on top of the left first finger.

Now take your stance at the ball. Your feet should be spread about the same width as your shoulders. Your left arm holding the club in a straight line should be just barely to the right of your left knee. That's the proper line for the ball, too. Checking it another way, the ball should be straight out from the inside of your left heel.

To help you get good balance, the toes of both feet should be pointed out—the right foot slightly to the right and the left foot a little more so to the left. Now check your aim on that target you picked before. Look at it. Is the face of the club aimed straight at it? This may be hard to tell, so here's how to double check yourself in practice. Have a friend lay a club down in front of your feet. If your stance is square—on line to the target—the club will be pointing at the spot you picked out before.

With the firm grip, a balanced stance, and a correct aim at the target, you are ready to hit the ball. Don't be nervous and don't be anxious—the ball won't run away. Get your eye steady over the ball and concentrate only on sweeping it right off the tee.

To keep you from becoming stiff before the backswing, try wriggling your wrists just a tiny bit. Move them a little forward just before taking the club back. This is called a forward press. It's nothing more than a miniature windup to get the muscles moving.

Take the club back slowly. This is so important that it's worth repeating to yourself over and over again when you are learning. Again, start the backswing slowly. Hurrying will just throw you off balance before you can get going.

A correct swing will move the club around the body and up at the same time. Keep your right elbow pointed at the ground all the time. If it flaps around up in the air, your swing will be ruined.

The driver is a long club, and you may wonder where the big wooden head is going on the backswing. Don't worry about it. Just take a natural turn as you bring the club back, and it will end up above your shoulder where it belongs.

With a good backswing most of the battle is won. As you bring the club down shove your weight over on the left foot and pull down with the left hand. But keep the wrists cocked until you are near the ball; then snap them as if you were cracking a bull whip.

Throughout the swing your head doesn't do a thing. If it moves to the side or if you look up to see where the ball is going before you've even hit it, you won't hit it at all. Keeping your head still is probably more important than any part of the swing itself.

With the longer wood club and full swing you must follow through after hitting the ball. That means your hands will take the club on around the left side of your body and up high over your left shoulder. That's when your head will come up, and not before. This follow-through is a natural result of a smooth, solid swing, just as when a baseball pitcher throws a high, hard one.

Don't worry about how your finish will look, though. A good finish is the result, not a cause, of a good swing.

These action photos of the player hitting a tee shot show: 1. At address, weight is balanced, knees bent, eyes over ball.

2. Starting the backswing, club is kept low to ground.

3. Wrists start to bend when club reaches waist level.

4. At top of backswing, left shoulder is under the chin, left knee bent.

5. Starting downswing, weight shifts over to left side.

6. The wrists straighten out and club comes into the ball in a sweep.

7. The head doesn't come up until ball is well on the way.

8. At the finish, the body faces the hole and hands bring club up high.

HOW TO HIT THE FAIRWAY WOODS

Even if you have only a few clubs when you start playing golf, your set should include at least one other wood besides a driver.

The fairway woods—numbers two, three, four and up—are important to the golf game of an average or beginning player. Their purpose is much the same as the driver: to get distance. The only real difference is that you use them to hit such shots off the ground after you are off the tee and somewhere down the fairway.

How do you know when to use a wood, as opposed to the more helpful-looking irons? There are two points to check on before pulling out the wood to hit a fairway shot, or occasionally one out of the rough. First, is the distance to the green too far to cover with an iron shot? You learn the answer with experience, but at first you will probably be using woods for any shot of more than 150 yards. But the ball must also be sitting up in the grass enough to enable you to hit it easily with a wood.

The higher number woods help you hit a long, straight shot off grass. They are a bit shorter in length than the number one wood. A shorter club is easier to swing and easier to control. The club heads on the higher number woods are a bit smaller so that you can sweep them through the grass with a minimum drag. Also, the loft on the hitting face has more of an angle as the club numbers get higher to

A new view of action shows how wood hits ball off the fairway: 1. Getting ready to swing, the left arm and club are in line with ball.

2. On the backswing, the right knee moves to point at right one.

3. The club is at its highest point in the swing and left arm is firm.

4. Coming down again, the right elbow stays close to the body. 5. The hands lead the club until they let loose. 6. The club picks the ball off the grass perfectly with eyes still on it.

make it easier for you to get the ball up in the air.

Hitting a wood shot off a fairway is difficult for many golfers, even experienced ones. There are two reasons for this. Without a tee under the ball most average golfers lose confidence in their woods. Because they are anxious they try to hurry their swing or lift the ball in the air. Usually they hit it badly and it never gets off the ground.

Basically, the wood shot off the ground is the same as the tee shot. The grip is the same. You line up on your target in the same way with the feet square to the line.

There is, however, a minor but natural adjustment to make in your stance. Because the club is not so long as a number one wood, and therefore the circle made by the swing is not so wide, your feet should not be quite so far apart at address. Your feet should get closer in relation to the shaft length of your

7. Following through, both arms extend out toward the hole.

8. Most of the weight is over on the left leg at the finish.

woods and irons until with the shortest iron your feet should be only a few inches apart for a short shot.

When hitting the ball off a tee, your driver makes a sweep up through the ball and pushes it into the air. That is the reason you placed the ball forward in your stance—opposite the left heel. But when you are using the more lofted woods and are hitting off the ground, the club does not have the room to get under the ball and sweep it away. Instead, it must pick the ball off clean. Therefore, set your stance so that the ball position lines up more to the center. This way the club will contact the ball at the very bottom of the swing.

You should make no effort to swing differently on fairway wood shots than you did on the tee. Just concentrate on a smooth swing, a firm grip, and on keeping your head still over the ball.

No matter how much you practice your swing, many of your wood shots when you are learning won't be long or straight. It would be a miracle if they were. Sad to say, many things can happen if that wood face doesn't hit the ball squarely.

It is better not to worry about the bad shots that you might make. Think only of swinging at the ball just as you do when clipping dandelions with a practice swing. Always keep your head still over the ball and look where the ball is going after, not before, you've hit it.

A slice is a beginning golfer's most common error. This is a shot that feels as if it is hit well, starts out straight, and then curves to the right, usually landing in the rough or behind a tree. Many things can cause a slice: a bad grip, lazy wrists, uncocking the wrists at the top of the backswing, leaving too much weight on the right leg, and other bad habits. The best cure is to concentrate on the basic fundamentals and keep working on them.

The opposite of a slice is a hook: a shot that starts out straight and then curves left. A hook may be caused by a grip with the hands turned too far to the right, or by raising the head, or by other small mistakes. For most people a hook is easier to cure than a slice.

You will also suffer through other shot problems that show up especially with fairway woods. These include hitting the ball on top so it never gets off the ground, hitting the ground behind the ball, hitting way under the ball causing it to go up very fast and come down like a bomb, and hitting the ball off the toe end of the club.

Again, the best solution is to follow the fundamentals of instruction. All golfers hit poor shots at times. But practice and experience will make errors less frequent.

Before deciding to use a wood for a fairway shot be sure that the lie of the ball is reasonably good. When playing in the fairway off the top of short, thick turf, conditions are in your favor. But if the ball is nestled down in clover or sitting on bare dirt where a wood can't glide smoothly into the back of the ball, use an iron instead.

The field where you practice may be level, but not many golf courses are. Often when the ball is sitting up nicely in the grass you find yourself standing on a slope. Some adjustments have to be made in order to hit the ball properly.

If the slope is sidehill, the ball will either be above or below your feet. If above, you must stand farther away to give the club room to swing. Aim to the right of your target, because the ball will tend to go with the hill. With the ball below your feet, you stand closer to the ball and aim left. If you are shooting up a hill, play the ball farther to the front of your stance because the club will reach the ground later.

Shooting downhill, the ball should be aligned more off the right foot. Normally you should not try to hit a wood from a downhill lie.

All of these situations will cause you problems sooner or later. Experience will teach you to solve them one by one. But meanwhile they will give you a taste of the challenge that makes golf so much fun.

HOW TO HIT THE IRONS

In baseball, tennis, and hockey, the stick for hitting the ball always looks the same. Except for a small difference in weight and length, for instance, every baseball player swings the same kind of bat. But golf clubs have two different sorts of heads—wood and iron (actually steel with chrome plate). This confuses many beginners. They don't know which kind of club to use for certain shots. They try to swing differently for woods than for irons. This confusion never ends for many golfers and they tend to favor either an iron or a wood whenever they play.

From the beginning, then, you should learn to regard both irons and woods as equally helpful clubs to use. At first you will have trouble hitting good shots consistently with all your clubs. But try not to favor one sort over the other.

In hitting irons, you shouldn't swing any differently than you did with woods. But as you familiarize yourself with your irons, remember these two points: First, although the long, heavy-head wood clubs are made to give maximum distance within the width of the fairway, the shorter, precision-honed irons are designed to get the ball on the green and close to the hole. Accuracy, not distance (except what comes without strain), is all important in iron play.

Second, the biting blade of an iron is made to get the shot up in the air if you hit down on the ball. This means that the swing first contacts the ball, then the ground, taking a divot of dirt after the ball has been sent on its way.

A full set of golf clubs might consist of as many as ten irons, numbers one to nine, plus a heavy-bladed sand wedge. But your first set of clubs will only contain some of these. For instruction purposes, the irons are usually divided into three groups: long, medium, and short. This refers both to the club length and the distances they are supposed to hit the ball. A beginner's set might have just a four or five iron, and an eight or nine iron; that is enough both to learn and to enjoy the game.

With a full set, or even with four or more irons, you often have a problem of deciding which club to use. In the long run this is something only you can decide according to the shot you must make. Basically, each club is supposed to hit a ball about ten yards more or less than the club next to it. So if after some practice you figure you can hit a five iron 140 yards with your best shot, then you know that a six iron should go about 130 yards, and so on. But even knowing this, you still have to learn to judge the distance to each green as you play. More important, you must hit the shot well to get that distance.

All irons are played basically alike. Only the length and loft of the face are changed to help you swing the same but get different lengths and heights to your shots. In a well-hit shot, the blade bites down on the back of the ball, pinching it, giving it backspin, and making it come down with a bite when it reaches the green.

Just as you made only slight adjustments between hitting a drive and a fairway wood so are there only minor changes between preparing to hit a wood and an iron. The grip is still the same, always the same. As each iron becomes shorter the closer you should align the ball to your body. But by just letting your

This is an action series on how to hit a six iron: 1. The club is shorter so the ball is closer to the body than with wood. 2. Going back, the club blade and wrists are still in line.

arms hang naturally in front of you, you will always have the right position. Pay attention, however, to your feet.

As the club and the shot become shorter, your stance should become narrower. In other words, the feet should be closer together for a six iron shot than for a three iron shot. Also, the left foot may be angled more to the left as the stance gets closer to-

3. Club is taken almost straight up when it reaches waist height.

4. At highest point, both feet are flat on the ground.

gether. Finally, for shorter shots, the position of the ball moves slightly closer to the right foot. All of these adjustments come naturally with experience. They increase the chances of an accurate shot with the shorter clubs.

The wrists and the control they provide are important to good iron shots. They must be kept firm both on the backswing and at impact with the ball.

5. Coming down, the wrists are just about to uncock here.

6. The right leg is shoving the weight over to the left ahead of club.

Looseness in the wrists or grip, either at the top or at impact, will make the shot lose power, direction, or both.

Beginners often try to scoop up the ball with their irons. They flip the wrists in attempting to pick the ball off the ground. Usually the result is a topped ball that never gets into the air. Remember, to get the ball up, you must hit down. This is as true with a

7. Right at impact, the club hits the ball, then digs through grass.

8. Going through, the right shoulder passes under the chin.

two iron as it is with a nine iron.

You will often have to use an iron to hit the ball out of rough grass or in awkward positions from holes or from hillsides. The iron blades will always do the job if you give them a chance.

In heavy rough, your main object is to get out of trouble, out on the fairway, and toward the hole. Don't use a wood or even a four or five iron that won't get the ball up out of the weeds in a hurry. Instead, take a seven iron or even a nine, and hit down hard to lift the ball up fast.

On hillside iron shots the principles are the same as with fairway woods. If you are on the side of a hill, with the ball above you, stand farther from the ball than normal. It is very easy to pull the ball left in such a shot, so aim to the right of your target. With the ball below your feet, aim to the left. When shooting uphill, take a lower number club but play the ball more forward in your stance so as to carry the upslope. Heading downhill, take a club with more loft and play it close to the right foot to keep from topping it into the level ground ahead.

Always remember to keep your hands firm, your head down, and your weight moving smoothly to your left as you hit into the ball. The club head will do the rest.

Since the irons are made to deliver a ball to the green, and since the shot to the green is a key one no matter what the distance, practice your irons as much as possible. Par golf allows only one approach shot per hole. Make that one count.

Closeups of feet and ball positions for a long iron and short iron shot. Feet are wider apart for long iron to aid balance. Ball is played farther to player's right with short iron to make sure club hits ball on downswing.

HOW TO USE THE WEDGE

Every beginning golfer should make friends early with his nine iron, or sand wedge, or both if the two of them are in his set. These clubs will save you strokes time after time if you work with them and get the feel of what they can do.

From 100 yards on in to the hole—as close as five yards off the green, in a trap, out of the rough, uphill or downhill—your shortest, most-lofted club is the weapon to use. At least while you are still learning you will probably need it on almost every hole. Soon, because you have come to know it so well and because hitting it takes the least physical effort and easiest swing of all, you will be making fine shots with your nine iron or wedge.

Shots with these clubs demand only a short swing. At the top, the hands need not be any higher than the shoulders, even for a full shot. And the swing is only half that long for short shots of twenty to fifty yards. You won't need to shift your weight back and forth, or turn your body at all. From the start the weight stays firm but slightly over on the left side. The wrists and arms alone are adequate for a short swing to make a short shot.

The best adjective to describe a well-hit nine iron shot is "crisp". With firm wrists and weight moving slightly ahead of your swing to the left side, you must hit down solidly into the back of the ball. The club will then glide down into the turf, take a good-sized divot, and come up in a short follow-through.

The wedge stance is a compact position, in line with the change from woods to long irons to medium irons. The feet should be quite close together. The left foot is pulled back from the line to the target, to give the arms room to move through the ball. When you stand up to the ball, it should be almost opposite the right foot, with the hands ahead to get them ready to hit down on the shot.

Without trying to describe every possible shot you may meet with your nine iron or wedge, we will explain the basic jobs it can do for you.

One is the high, back-spinning pitch shot from up to 100 yards away. This takes a full swing or nearly so, depending on the distance. The ball should fly high, come down on the green, and stop there.

From in closer, within ten to twenty-five yards of the green, a pitch is best made with a wedge. There are pitching wedges designed to do this job well. Such a club puts more backspin on the ball. You will soon learn to make the ball stop close to the hole after it hits the green.

From just off the green, or when there is some room between the edge and the hole, a chip-and-run shot is better. This is not much more than a hard putting swing. By keeping your hands well ahead of the club head when it hits the ball, the shot takes off low and rolls to the hole. If possible, aim to make sure that the ball does not hit the ground until it gets to the closely mowed green, where it is less likely to bounce or roll off line.

These action photos are of a chip shot with eight iron from near green: 1. Ball is played opposite the center of the feet at address.

2. Arms and wrists alone move the club on back-swing.

3. This is as far as the club has to be taken back.

4. The weight is shifting just a bit to left as club comes back down.

5. Hands are leading club and wrists are firm just before the hit.

6. Club hits down and pops the ball up out of the grass.

7. The head stays down until well after the ball is gone.

8. The club head follows straight toward the hole.

A ball in a sand bunker needs a heavy, open-faced club to help pop it out. Club must not touch the sand at address. Aim must be at a point about two inches in back of the ball.

These action photos show how a good swing pops the ball out of sand: 1. Ready to hit, clubhead is held back of ball at aiming point.

Frequently there is rough grass to the sides or in back of a green. A long shot that misses often winds up in such trouble. There your nine iron or wedge will get you up on the green. Just remember to hit down so that the ball will pop out. Don't try to scoop it. Remember, too, that a ball coming out of deep

2. With a short club, it is lifted straighter up than on other shots.

3. Eye is on point two inches behind ball at top of swing.

grass will have almost no backspin on it, so allow room for it to roll to the hole.

The worst spot to be in is a sand trap. Traps are common hazards around greens. They are made purposely to penalize a poor shot hit at the green. The sand wedge was invented about thirty years ago to make escape from traps easier.

If you get in the sand, don't be afraid of it. Even

4. Coming down, knees bend into a "sitting down" position. 5. The clubhead comes nearly straight down into the sand. 6. Going into and through the sand, the clubhead pops ball up and out.

if the ball is sitting down in a hole, and the fairway or green is two or three feet above you, concentrate only on getting out. The grip and swing will be the same as for a normal pitch shot off grass. But make these changes: first, open up the face of the club to the right so it lies flatter; second, play the ball opposite the left heel; finally, aim to hit about an inch behind the ball, into the sand. With an ordinary

7. Eye is still right on the spot where clubhead struck the sand.

8. Follow-through of club is shorter but hands are still solid.

smooth swing—be sure to follow all the way through under the ball—the force of the moving sand will push the ball up and out onto the green.

None of these short shots will automatically stop near the hole for you right away. This is a part of the game where experience and "touch" are your guides. Constant practice will help you lower your score faster.

HOW TO PUTT

Putting is often called a game within a game. Anyone can learn how to putt at least reasonably well even as a beginner. The skills and thinking involved are quite different from swinging and hitting a ball a considerable distance down the fairway. This is why some golfers who cannot shoot low scores are still good putters, and why a few good golfers are not even average putters.

Before you start worrying, though, let us tell you that putting is far easier to learn than a perfect golf swing. It probably won't take long before you are popping the ball into the hole as often as anyone you know.

First, however, you must learn how hard to hit the ball. As you play, luck will give you all kinds of putts—long, medium, short, uphill, downhill, sidehill. Learning how to hit each one comes only with experience. This skill is called the "feel of the green" and you must have it to be a good putter.

Right now, though, let's start at the beginning. The first and only piece of equipment you need is a putting club. It really does not matter what kind you use. It's what you do with it that counts.

If you have a chance to select a putter from the

Variations in style of putter blades are shown in this selection of new clubs. All are legal and any one may be right for you.

variety sold in pro shops, the decision will not be easy. The best way to make your choice is to take several out to the putting green and see how they feel to you.

There are at least four things to look for in a putter. The four should all make you feel comfortable as you hold it, swing it, and tap a ball with it. These qualities include the weight, balance of weight in the head, length of shaft, and type of grip.

In weight most putters are about the same. Unless you have small or weak hands, or the greens at your course are large and demand long putts, a light putter will help you learn the "feel" faster. The balance of weight is even more important; the club should feel good as you hold it and stroke the ball.

The length and grip should be fitted to your physical characteristics and habits if possible. If you are not too tall yet, you won't want to use one of the longer models. It would be hard to control. The grip on the club may be flat, round, square, or curved, made of leather, cork, or rubber. Pick up several and see what fits best in your hands.

How you grip a putter is also up to you. Because the putting stroke requires little physical action, the method of holding the club is secondary to an accu-

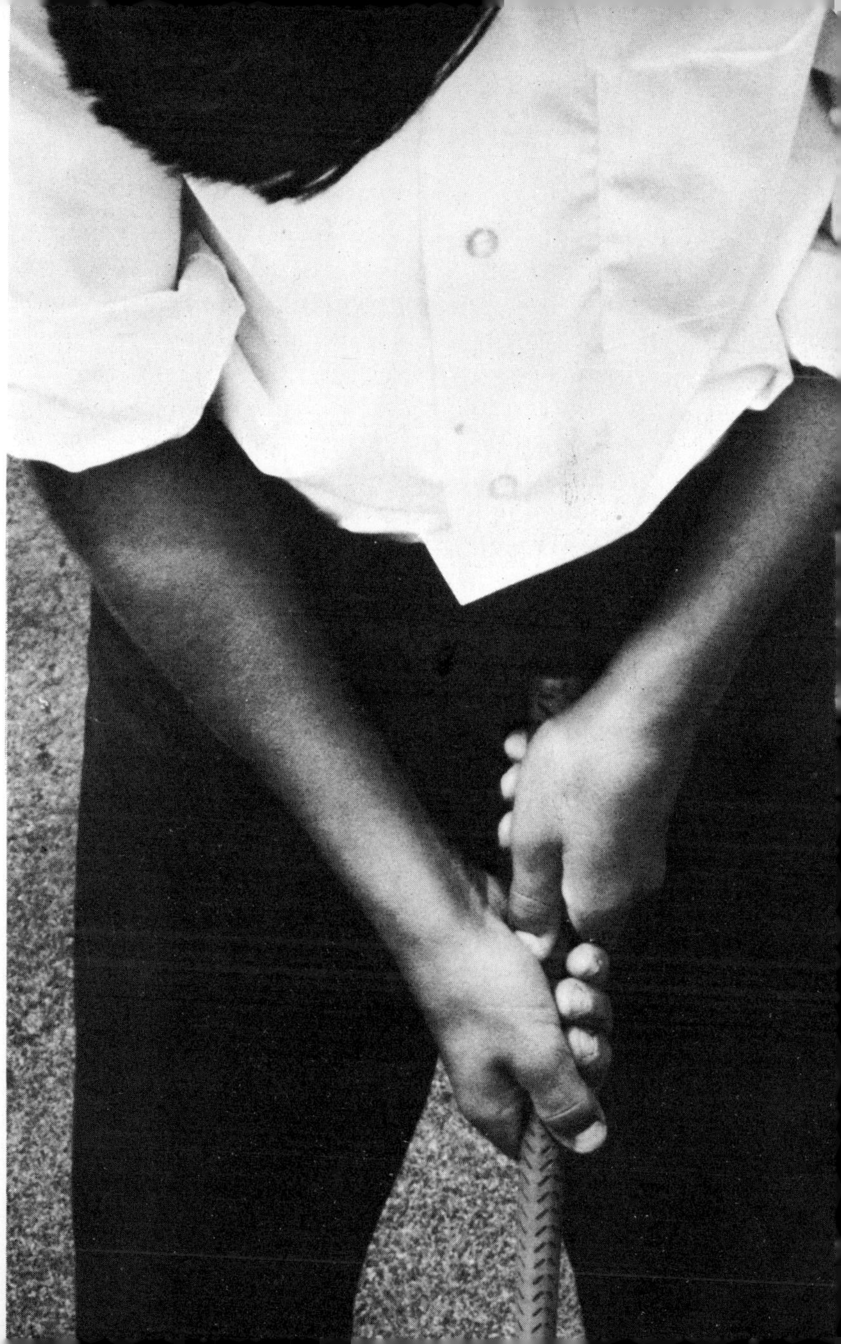

Grip for putting depends on what feels comfortable. This one is similar to regular golf grip, except that left thumb points straight down top of club shaft and back of hand faces hole.

Down on the green, a closeup of the putting stance shows feet close together, toes straight and square with the hole, ball opposite the inside of the left foot and lined up on the center of the putter blade.

ratc stroke. You do not have to use the normal overlapping grip; in fact, few golfers do.

The most popular is called the reverse overlapping. It's made by placing the left hand on the shaft so that the V between thumb and forefinger points at the left shoulder. Then the right hand goes on below so that the V points at the right shoulder. But instead of the little finger of the right hand being over the left forefinger, their positions reverse.

But if this is not comfortable for you, try something else. The baseball grip or the hands directly opposite with both thumbs on top of the grip may be better for you. There is one important principle to keep in mind, though. To help you develop a square stroke that will hit straight putts, always try to have the back of your left hand aiming straight at the hole.

There is no universal rule for how to stand, either. Just be sure you are comfortable. It doesn't matter if you keep both feet almost together or spread them way apart. Your weight may be balanced or mostly on the left foot. Most good golfers, however, line up their feet at right angles to the hole, have their weight just about on center, bend over so that their eyes are looking straight down on the ball, and keep their hands and elbows in close to their body.

The important key to success in getting ready to putt is to adopt a stance that will prevent you moving your head or body during the stroke. Staying in place is even more important on the green than on full golf shots. If you sway or move off center slightly, you will ruin a straight putting stroke.

The stroke itself should be simple and firm. Just take the club back smoothly, using the right wrist as a little hinge. Make it firm and not too fast. Then, in hitting the ball, the hinge closes again. This means the right hand just pops the ball. The left hand merely guides the club on line.

The tough part about hitting the ball square is to keep the putter blade in perfect line even on a short backswing. Be careful to look at the hole several

How the putter rolls the ball smoothly to the hole is demonstrated here: 1. Over the ball, hands and arms are close to body. 2. Starting backstroke, clubhead is kept low to the ground and square. 3. Right wrist is bending just a bit as left moves club back.

4. Even for this long putt the club just goes back to right foot. 5. Coming into the ball, the clubhead is as square as when it started. 6. The hands are just where they started as club contacts ball.

7. Clubhead is on upswing to give ball overspin on way to hole.

8. On the follow-through the left wrist breaks over and right moves under.

times to get it lined up right. Then, as you take the stroke, concentrate on keeping the putter blade low along the ground and your head steady over the ball.

If a putt is hit just right, the ball will have true overspin as it runs along the ground. If the blade does not hit the ball squarely, it will have a little sidespin. That's why a low, dead-center stroke is so important. It doesn't take much of an error to throw the ball off line, even though the cup is more than twice as large as a golf ball.

As you gain experience and confidence you will find that many putts you hit well go straight into the cup. But, alas, you will also discover that grain in the grass and humps in the green often turn the ball away from the cup. In fact, you will learn that very few putts will stay exactly on line to the cup even if you hit the ball straight.

That's why you must learn to "read" the greens. This simply means taking a look at the area between your ball and the cup. At least the hills, if any, are obvious. You must allow for a "break" in the roll of the ball, following the slope after you hit it.

But even on absolutely flat ground the character of the grass can cause problems. Even on the best-kept greens, the grass is unlike your smooth rug at home. You may want to practice your stroke in your

Lining up a putt, the typical position is to get down near the ground to see any hills or valleys between ball and hole.

living room, but you won't get the feel of "grain" and "speed" until you putt on a real green.

Grain is simply the direction grass tends to lean, because of sun, wind, erosion, or slope. If you look closely at the grass, particularly near the cup where your ball slows down and is affected most, you can usually see the grain. The ball will tend to roll in the direction the grass leans.

On a green recently mowed you can stand behind your ball, look toward the cup, and see patterns where the mower cut. From where you stand, the light streaks are with the grain, the dark streaks against the grain. You will soon learn to hit your ball a little harder or easier than normal to make up for this factor.

Above all, you must have confidence to be a good putter. To gain that you must practice, you must concentrate, you must try very hard, and you must not become afraid of missing.

Try to follow this routine. Look at your putt and the line from behind the ball. Pick a spot to aim at, either part of the cup or a spot to one side if you have to allow for considerable break. Take two or three practice swings. Stand up to the ball and hit it where you aimed it. Never change your mind about where or how hard to hit it halfway through the stroke.

If you miss, forget it and try harder next time. Just keep visualizing every putt going into the hole. Pretty soon many of them will be doing just that.

MANNERS ON THE GOLF COURSE

With a little study and practice of the fundamentals you should by now have a good idea of how the game of golf is played. Your improvement from here on in depends on how hard you work at it.

But to be a golfer you need to know more than how to hit a ball. As a game, golf has rules. As a competitive sport, golf demands good sportsmanship. You must learn and obey the rules and code of good conduct in order really to know the game.

The basic rules of golf are actually very simple. First, play the ball as it lies at all times, meaning don't touch it from the time you place it on a tee until you take it out of the cup. Second, count every stroke, even misses.

There will be questions from time to time that can't be solved by these two commandments. But somewhere in the little rule book for golf there is an answer. So before you play very often, and especially in tournaments, buy a rule book from the professional at your course, read it, and carry it in your bag.

The unwritten rules are also extremely important. These are the little do's and don'ts that make it easier for everyone to enjoy golf as a social game and yet play without interference from their partners or

For safety and courtesy it is important to stand back away from a player who is hitting, and neither move nor talk.

opponents. The object of these rules is good sportsmanship and fair play.

Some of the important points of good etiquette are: Don't talk or move, including taking practice swings, when anyone near you is addressing or hitting the ball.

Don't stand either directly in back of or in front of the line of flight while anyone is hitting a shot.

Don't step in the line of someone's putt, between his ball and the hole, even before he is ready to putt. The footprint will dent the grass and keep the ball from rolling smoothly.

Don't let your shadow fall across anyone's ball or his line to the hole while he is putting.

Don't hit your ball until you are sure no one ahead of you could get hit, even by your longest or wildest shot.

Don't hit your ball while playing with others until everyone else farther from the hole has already hit.

Don't pull your cart or drag your bag through a sand bunker or over a green.

Don't forget to replace your divots in the fairway and rough, and smooth down any holes your ball makes in the greens.

Don't hold up players behind you if you are slow or are looking for a lost ball. Wave at them to go on

If your ball is lost, wave to players behind to go on by while you look.

To keep the golf course in good shape for everyone, be sure to put back divots you might dig up while hitting a shot.

Leave your bag, and cart, too, a good distance off greens when you get ready to putt.

A ball coming down hard on a soft green leaves a hole. Fix it with the point of a tee to leave the green smooth for others.

Hitting out of a sand bunker, you will make a big hole. Smooth it out before you leave.

The player who is the most distance from the hole always plays first. Here the player is getting his ball out of his opponent's way by marking it with a coin until it is his turn to play.

past you, and wait until they are out of range before you shoot.

Don't walk ahead off the tee or leave the green until every player in your group has hit or putted out.

Don't litter the course with trash.

Most important of all, don't lose your temper and bang your clubs on the ground or use bad language. Everyone makes a bad shot now and then, and getting mad about it does no good. Just try harder on the next shot.

As you become a better player, you will probably want to enter tournaments. Certainly you will also want to try out for your school's golf team. Playing on a team combines the fun of trying to do well on

When another person putts, a courteous player stands silently off to the side, also making sure his shadow does not cross the hole or in line with the putt.

your own and trying to help your school win.

Don't be afraid to enter tournaments, no matter what you shoot. (Both junior and open tournaments are arranged so that you will be playing in divisions with and against golfers who score about what you do.) Such competition will give you reason to do your best on every shot. You will probably play your best golf, and your scores may improve.

Rules and etiquette are doubly important in competition. Knowing them will assure fair play at all times. You can be penalized or even disqualified for breaking certain rules. And ignorance of a rule is no excuse.

The boy or girl who plays tournament golf must learn to be a good loser as well as a good winner. No one wins every time in golf. Your attitude about yourself and about your opponents is important. A humble champion is much more popular than a cocky, bragging champion. A proud loser who congratulates the winner and vows to himself to do better next time is more popular than a sorehead.

Once you start playing golf, you probably won't ever want to quit. Most people find it fun and challenging, no matter what score they shoot. Keep this attitude in mind. Play the game for all it's worth, but always enjoy yourself.

GLOSSARY OF GOLF TERMS

ADDRESS—A position with the feet and club placed ready to hit the ball.

APRON—Well-kept, trimmed fairway grass within about six feet of the green.

BIRDIE—A score that is one less than the rated par for a hole.

BOGEY—A score one over the rated par for a hole.

BREAK—A sidehill roll of the ball on a green caused by its contour.

BUNKER—An area of bare ground, usually a hole, and usually covered with sand; sometimes called a sand trap.

CADDIE—A person who carries or handles a player's clubs during play.

CARRY—Distance a ball travels in the air after it is hit.

CASUAL WATER—Any temporary accumulation of water, such as snow or puddles from rain, which is not a regular water hazard but interferes with play.

COURSE—The whole area within which play is permitted.

CUP—The metal or plastic liner within a hole on the green; sometimes used to mean the hole.

DOUBLE BOGEY—A score two over the rated par for a hole.

EAGLE—A score that is two less than the rated par for a hole.

FAIRWAY—The area of mowed grass between the tee and the green.

FLAGSTICK—The straight stick, usually with a numbered cloth attached, which stands in the center of the hole to mark its location from a distance.

FORE—The most common word used by a player who is about ready to hit or who has hit to warn players ahead of him to watch out for the ball heading their way.

FORECADDIE—A person employed during tournaments to indicate to players the locations of their balls.

FOURSOME—A match of two teams of two players each.

FRINGE—A width of fairway-length turf around the edge of the green.

GREEN—Short name for putting green—the closely mowed area around the hole especially prepared for putting.

GROUND RULES—At a golf course, certain instructions governing play and warning of hazards.

GRIP—To take hold of the club before the stroke; also the term for the wrapped part of the club made to hold it.

GROUND UNDER REPAIR—Any part of the course marked to show construction or an unusually rough area; a ball in it may be lifted out.

HANDICAP—A number indicating the relative ability of a player, based on the difference between his best average score and par over eighteen holes.

HAZARD—A bunker or water area such as a pond or a stream.

HEAD—In golf, the large part of the club made for hitting the ball.

HEEL—The area of the club head facing nearest the shaft; also, to hit a ball off that part of the club.

HOLE—The objective of the ball on each green, 4¼ inches in diameter, 4 inches deep; also, one of the eighteen parts of a round of golf.

HOLE HIGH—A shot which has come to rest about equal distance with the hole on the green, but off to the side.

HONOR—A player or team hitting first from the tee because of winning the previous hole.

HOOK—A shot curving from right to left in flight.

IRON—A club with a head usually made of steel in a blade form, relatively narrow from face to back.

LIE—How the ball sits on the grass in the fairway or rough areas.

LIFT—To pick up a ball and move it in the fairway, out of the rough or from a hazard, in accordance with rules allowing such an act in particular situations.

LINKS—Originally a term for a seaside golf course; sometimes used to mean any golf course.

LIP—The edge of the hole; also, the edge of a sand bunker.

LOFT—Angle of the face of a club, which determines the approximate height and distance a club will hit a ball.

MATCH PLAY—A game in which one side plays another hole by hole, with the winner being the one that wins the most holes.

MEDAL PLAY—A term for stroke play, in which many players compete on a basis of total score for nine or more holes.

OBSTRUCTION—Anything man-made, built or left on the course.

OUT OF BOUNDS—Ground on which play is prohibited, marked by stakes or a fence.

PAR—The rated score for a hole or a round which the best players should make, allowing two putts on each green.

PENALTY STROKE—An extra stroke added to a score under certain rules, either for hitting the ball into an unplayable position or for breaking the rules.

PIN—A slang term for flagstick.

PROVISIONAL BALL—A second ball which is played after the first has been hit out of bounds or lost, until the first is either found or proved unplayable.

PULL—A shot hit to the left of where it was aimed.

PUSH—A shot hit to the right of where it was aimed.

PUTTER—A club with an almost straight face designed to hit the ball on the putting green.

READING THE GREEN—To look at the slope and grass on a green to determine how to hit a putt.

ROUGH—The unmowed and usually unkempt areas of grass and trees bordering the fairways.

SHAFT—The length of hollow steel connecting the club head and the area of the grip.

SHANK—To hit a ball with an iron at the base of the shaft where it curves into the head, causing it to go at an odd angle to the right.

SLICE—A shot curving from left to right in flight.

STANCE—The placement of the feet in addressing the ball.

STROKE—A forward movement of the club with the intention of moving the ball.

STROKE PLAY—A game in which all players compete based on total score for nine or more holes; sometimes called medal play.

STYMIE—Under old rules, a situation in which one ball blocks another's line to the hole; more common now to describe a situation in which a tree blocks a shot to the green.

TEE—Short name for teeing ground, the starting place for each hole; also, the small wooden peg used to hold the ball off the ground for the first shot on a hole.

TIE—The result when two sides shoot the same score on one hole or for a round.

TIGHT—A slang term meaning the ball is either sitting low in the grass or is very near the hole.

TOE—The area at the end of the club head; also, to hit a ball off the end of the club.

TRAP—A slang term for a sand bunker.

UNPLAYABLE—A bad position for the ball, making it impossible to hit and forcing the player to take a penalty stroke.

WINTER RULES—Allowing players to improve the position of their ball on the fairway; not actually allowed by the *Rules of Golf*.

WOOD—A club with a head usually made of wood in a round, broad form.